WHO S' MY PIE?

How to manage priorities, boundaries and expectations

Joe Cheal

Publishing

Published in England
by GWiz Publishing
(A division of The GWiz Learning Partnership)
Oakhurst, Mardens Hill, Crowborough, E. Sussex. TN6 1XL
Tel (+44) 1892 309205

info@gwiztraining.com

www.gwiztraining.com

First published 2014.
10 9 8 7 6 5 4 3 2

© Joe Cheal 2014

Cover illustrations and 'Walter' character by Rob Banbury
All illustrations © 2014

ISBN: 978-0-9548800-6-4

Contents

Foreword   vii

1   A First Slice of Pie   **1**

Session 1: Walter learns some home truths about his use of time   7

2   A Second Slice of Pie   **19**

Session 2: Walter learns the true nature of assertiveness, boundaries and expectations   23

3   A Third Slice of Pie   **39**

Session 3: Walter learns how his time is being used and how he could gain more control of it   43

4   A Fourth Slice of Pie   **63**

Session 4: Walter learns about prioritising   67

5   A Fifth Slice of Pie   **83**

Session 5: Walter learns the importance of communication   87

6   A Sixth Slice of Pie   **99**

Session 6: Walter discovers the 'Holy Grail of Delegation'   103

7   A Final Slice of Pie   **125**

Notes & Further Reading   **131**

About the Author   **133**

Acknowledgements

I would like to thank the following people for their help and support along the way:

Melody Cheal... *For her feedback and her marvellous ideas.*

Simon Deards... *For his insights, feedback and encouragement.*

Rob Banbury... The Master Illustrator... *For his extra-ordinary ability to draw so much into his animations.*

All the people on courses over the last 20 years who have asked questions and given me ideas about time management... particularly what works and what doesn't... *in the real world*!

JC 2014

In Memory of the original Walter... My Dad.

Foreword

About Time

Whilst I am eternally fascinated by people, I am equally compelled by how people relate to time.

We tend to treat time as something real and tangible but really it is a construct, a convenient way of measuring the processes and cycles of life.

We tend to treat time as if it is a constant, and yet Einstein pointed out that time is relative. A minute with a wonderful person will probably feel different to a minute spent sitting on a hot stove. Indeed, I hear people say (including myself) that time seems to be speeding up. The distance between each birthday gets shorter and shorter! Of course, each ongoing year is relatively shorter compared to the rest of our life.

We will often be 'up against the clock', hurrying from one thing to another. James Gleick, in his book *Faster* calls this 'hurry sickness.' People talk of being busy as if it is a necessity in today's world (both in busi-ness and at home). Busy is the norm. When someone asks you "how's work", try replying "not very busy" and then watch for the pitying looks. Eckhart Tolle talks of watching people rushing from one thing to another in order to get there sooner.

This 'battle' with time is fine to a point. However, we know it has a down side... Stress and anxiety are rife within organisations. People expected to do 'more for less' as they are asked to add another pile of stuff to their already burgeoning to-do lists. Something has to give... and personally, I do not wish it to be the wellbeing of the individuals involved.

So I got curious. Is there a way to slow it down... to 'stop the world'? Is there a way we can become more purposeful and hence more meaningful? Is there a way to feel fulfilled instead of 'full-filled'?

Having run hundreds of 'Time Management' courses, I came to the (obvious) conclusion that we cannot 'manage' time. We can only manage ourselves and our activities within the time available. This changes things because it means we are no longer the 'victim' to time, but taking responsibility for ourselves within a given context.

In these courses, I would hear people talking about their 'real world', where many of the standard time management tips didn't work (often because they didn't have time to implement them!) And so, over time, I built upon existing ideas and developed my own 'reality based' approaches. I wanted to meet the real world head on and find some tools and strategies that reflected the environment of chaos, complexity, ambiguity and overload.

Having dropped the notion of 'managing time', I have replaced it with 'managing priorities, boundaries and expectations' (hence the subtitle of this book).

About Who Stole My Pie

Whilst we may measure time in quantity (seconds, minutes, days etc), it is still rather abstract to our way of thinking. In order to 'get real' about time, it is helpful to make our time more tangible. Perhaps think of it as a set of coins or counters (of which there is a limited supply each day)... or a pie.

Walter brings a pie in to work each day for his lunch. Other people see the pie and want a bit. His pie is being eaten into.

Walter has a set amount of time each day to get his work done. Other people see that time and want a bit. His time is being eaten into.

Fortunately for Walter, help is at hand...

A First Slice of Pie

Who Stole My Pie

It was the kind of discovery that you make once or twice in a lifetime.

For Walter, it was the kind of discovery that someone else usually discovered first. This time, however, *he was first*... and it was his secret.

One morning, two things coincided and they changed his life forever. For a reason only known to Walter's curiosity, he decided to take an alternative route to work. As he turned down an unfamiliar backstreet, he realised all of a sudden that he had forgotten his lunch.

At that moment, the clouds parted and beam of sunlight illuminated the words '*PIE IN 'ERE*'. As he stood for a moment and gazed at the sign, little did he know that he had discovered the most wonderful pie shop in the world. The aroma was enticing and he felt compelled to go in.

Who Stole My Pie

Within minutes, he was on his way again, ready for work with a pie in his bag and a spring in his step.

That lunchtime turned out to be a joyful experience. One piece of pie and he was hooked. Delicious!

He also noticed a few glances his way as people looked sadly at their own lunch and then longingly at his.

As the weeks went by and he brought in a pie each day, it didn't take long for others to begin to ask for a nibble and a taste. But nibbles soon became bites and tastes soon became slices.

As a 'people person', Walter was happy to share his pie with others. He smiled at the joy it brought them and he was becoming quite the centre of attention. However, as the days passed and the word spread, Walter found that he was going home hungry as he was getting less and less pie for himself. He even tried buying two pies each day. This worked for a bit but the pies soon disappeared. Most people would ask first, but then others began to help themselves.

Eventually, there came a day when he went to get his lunchtime pie and found it *all* gone. And that was the day that he finally (and completely) lost it. From the office kitchen came a Walter shaped cry... "Who Stole My Pie???"

The 'pie' related meltdown was the last straw as far as Walter's manager was concerned. Once upon a time, Walter had been a productive member of staff but in the past few months he had been complaining of being under pressure and feeling overloaded. He had been missing deadlines and not checking his work before sending it out to the customers.

The Manager had overheard Walter saying to a colleague: "I can only do one thing at a time." The problem was... he wasn't even doing that one thing very well.

The Manager wondered: "What is he doing with his time?" and then she had an idea.

In the company there was a chap known simply as the Doctor. The Doctor was a problem solver, a trouble-shooter and a mentor around the business. He was particularly helpful when it came to matters of time. So she booked Walter in to see him.

Who Stole My Pie

Session One

Walter learns some home truths about his use of time

Walter dashed in to the Doctor's office and sat down in a rush.

"Welco-" began the Doctor.

"I must keep this quick," interrupted Walter speaking ten to the dozen. "I don't have time to be here. I've got too much to do. People are relying on me. I don't want to let them down. I'm under so much pressure."

The Doctor responded immediately, joining Walter in his fast pace manner. "So you want to be helpful to others?"

"Of course!" said Water abruptly, as if anything otherwise would be nonsense.

"So if you are under so much pressure that it leads to you being off with stress, how helpful will *that* be to others?" asked the Doctor, maintaining the same frantic pace as Walter.

Walter paused for a moment then said: "If I was off with stress, they wouldn't be able to get their job done."

"So you agree that it would be good to find a way to reduce the pressure and handle things differently to how you are doing them now?" asked the Doctor, beginning to slow down.

Who Stole My Pie

"I guess so yes," Walter agreed.

"So," began the Doctor, pausing before continuing. "Let's start with this… Would you agree that there is a finite amount of time to get things done? You have thirty-seven and a half hours in the working week. That's just over twenty-two hundred minutes. Have you ever asked yourself: Where does the time go?"

"Of course!" moaned Walter.

"You need to make your time tangible," the Doctor explained. "Imagine you had ten pounds in coins at the start of the day and people kept asking you for a pound here and there. Would you hand it over without question?"

"I… well… no… but I'm the only one who can do it," cried Walter, his face contorting momentarily in a flash of anguish. "And it's always urgent!"

"Okay so let's put this to the test," said the Doctor reassuringly. "What happens when you are on holiday?"

"I can't take holidays," said Walter incredulously. "I've got too much to do."

"Well then, imagine that you are away for two weeks. Someone has something they would normally ask you to do. You are not there… so what do they do?"

Walter's face paled visibly at the thought. "Um. I don't know. There would be chaos! So much wouldn't get done. People would be waiting around for me to get back. My desk would be a pile of files and requests. My email box would jam up. People would get so angry with me."

"Really?" challenged the Doctor. "So they would simply leave it on your desk and wait?"

"Yes!" said Walter and inside he was thinking: *At last, he finally appears to understand the pickle I'm in.*

"Which means it's not as urgent as they say it is then," announced the Doctor leaning forward with a broad smile. "Particularly if they're happy to wait two whole weeks for you to handle it. And if it *was* genuinely urgent and had to be handled at that moment... what would they really do?"

"I guess they would do it themselves," said Walter suspiciously, as if unsure whether he was walking into a trap. "Or I guess they would find someone else to help them."

"Well *there's* a thought!" grinned the Doctor, his eyes gleaming. "You now have your first principle:

What would happen to this task if I was away for a couple of weeks?

This will give you an idea of how urgent it is *really* and it will give you a clue as to what alternatives they have instead of asking you. People take what's known as the 'path of least resistance'. If you've always said yes in the past... guess who they'll come to next time?"

Walter nodded. He figured that it was a rhetorical question.

Encouraged, the Doctor continued: "So ask yourself:

- *When does this need doing by? How urgent is it really?*
- *Who else can help?*
- *What could they do for themselves?"*

"So are you telling me not to help people anymore?" asked Walter, feeling a little confused. The idea of being unhelpful was a horrible thought.

"Not at all!" reassured the Doctor. "It's simply about helping people with the *right things* rather than with everything."

"But how do I know what the right things are?"

"Well let's look at how your time might be used. In the same way that *you* might use your own time effectively or ineffectively, so *other people* may try to use your time appropriately or inappropriately. 'Appropriate' would mean asking you to do what you are paid to do within reasonable timescales. For example, let me show you." The Doctor wrote out two columns as follows:

HOW OTHERS USE YOUR TIME	
Inappropriate	Appropriate
✘ Managers dumping tasks on you that you are not properly briefed/trained to do. ✘ Colleagues getting you to do tasks that belong to them. ✘ People wanting to gossip	✔ Managers delegating tasks that you are trained to do. ✔ Colleagues passing work to you that is part of your job. ✔ Colleagues asking you for advice/input. ✔ People involving you in relevant decisions/plans.

"The question you may want to ask yourself is:

Does this help me do what I'm actually paid to do?

And for every task that heads in your direction ask:

Does this task really belong to me?"

Walter looked at the floor for a moment and muttered: "Sometimes part of the task is mine but I end up doing all of it."

"And I'm sure that's okay sometimes. But given what we've been talking about, how might you handle that differently if you need to?" the Doctor asked.

"I guess I could do the bit that's mine and then give it back?" suggested Walter.

"Excellent!" exclaimed the Doctor. "Do the bit that helps you to fulfil the purpose of your job and *then* let them fulfil the purpose of their own job."

"Purpose?" asked Walter, eyebrows raised. "What does that mean?"

"Basically, it's why you are employed. It's the reason you are paid."

"Huh?" said Walter, one eyebrow raised this time.

The Doctor smiled patiently and asked Walter what his job role was. Walter replied, giving him an overview.

"Okay, so you've told me what you do... now why do you do it? You do what you do in order to what?"

"I do what I do in order to get paid," said Walter... then stared blankly at the Doctor as if waiting for another question.

"Okay," continued the Doctor. "What would happen if you stopped doing your job? In fact... what would happen if *your job stopped*... and no-one replaced you doing what you do? If you are part of a team that does the same thing... then the whole team stops. All the tasks you are employed to do won't get done. It would be like a hole in the system. What would be the impact on those around you? To other departments? To your customers? To the organisation? What would happen straight away and then what would be the longer term ripple effects?"

Walter thought about it for a moment and then took a minute or so to tell the Doctor all the terrible things that would happen and all the awful things that would go wrong if he didn't do his job.

"So," surmised the Doctor, "your job has a purpose... in part to prevent those things you just told me about from happening! So, now, how would you describe the purpose of your job?"

Walter again considered the question and told the Doctor the purpose of his job. He then finished with an observation: "So this is really about time management?"

"Possibly," conceded the Doctor. "Although you don't really manage *time*... you manage yourself and your environment. Today we've looked at how you work with others. We've started exploring the nature of boundaries. Perhaps you might want to think about the tasks you do currently. You can carry on business as usual but keep a note of which tasks are *really* yours and which tasks really belong to others."

"*Keep a note,*" summarised Walter as he wrote it down on his pad.

The Doctor looked at Walter for a bit, obviously thinking something through. Then he nodded as if coming to a decision. "What I want to help you do here is '*stop the world*'."

"As in 'stop the world I want to get off'?" asked Walter.

"As in step back and look at your job from an objective perspective... to get off the treadmill and see how you are using your time... to come up with ideas as to how you can make your work-life a happier place."

Walter seemed a little confused. "But you said 'stop the world'."

"Indeed," agreed the Doctor. "A good friend of mine talks about 'freezing the spinning plates' or 'freeze-framing all the balls that are in the air'. That way he can stop, see what's going on and make some considered decisions about: what to do next, what can wait and what might need addressing as part of a bigger issue."

"Nice idea!" said Walter. He often spoke of trying to keep all the plates spinning and he liked the thought of them all frozen there in suspended animation. It made sense that he could

then prioritise and organise himself. It gave him a strange sense of relief... he could stop and breath.

"When you step into my office," said the Doctor. "It is time to *stop the world*. Remember... *Simon says!*"

Walter sat listening... but realised that the Doctor had stopped talking... so he just stared at the Doctor instead.

Since the Doctor was staring back, Walter asked: "Is that it? Is it over? Are we done already?"

"I thought you said you didn't have much time!" smiled the Doctor.

"Yes... of course... I don't... not much time at all..." responded Walter, somewhat disappointedly. "But this was getting interesting... I thought we'd only just begun."

"Indeed we have!" agreed the Doctor, gesturing towards the door. "See you soon."

After Walter had left his office, the Doctor grinned. "Yes indeed, we have only just begun."

Walter's Notes

<u>Make my time more tangible... Maybe time is like a Pie!</u>
Think of my time in terms of a pie. I start each day with a pie. Every task I need to do is a slice of pie. The bigger the task, the bigger the slice. And I only have one pie!
- What size slice does someone want from me?
- Do I have enough left?

<u>Should I be handing out slices of time to everyone?</u>
If someone is asking me to do something for them, what would happen if I wasn't here to ask?
- How urgent is it really?
- How else might they get it done? Who else could help them?

<u>Right Pie, Right Time!</u>
If someone is asking me to do something for them, am I the right person to be asking?
- Does it help me achieve the purpose of my job (i.e. what I'm actually employed to do)?
- Does this use my time effectively?

I need to help people with the *right* things rather than with everything!

Who Stole My Pie

A Second Slice of Pie

Who Stole My Pie

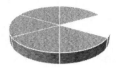

Walter was raging: "It is *my* pie. It belongs to me. I bought it. I own it. Get off! IT IS MY PIE!"

Enough was enough!! Walter was getting fed up with people getting fed up on his pies. It was time to say: "No!"

No, No, NO!!

When people said "can I have some of your pie because I'm hungry", Walter would reply: "No! Your hunger is not my fault and not my problem."

When people said "but I forgot my lunch", he would reply: "No! You need to plan your food better. Don't keep stealing mine."

So, people took to nibbling teeny tasters of the pie and 'liberating' bits of the crust. This all added up to larger pieces of pie missing. It seemed that the more people took... then the more people took!

To combat this gradual pie-loss and to make his point clearly, Walter wrapped his pie up and stuck a flag in it that read:

"This pie belongs to Walter. Keep off!"

Although the wrapping and flagging system was working, it meant his pie going rather soft and mushy by lunchtime. Still... better a mushy pie than no pie at all. And at least no-one else could have it!!

It was no coincidence that Walter found himself eating alone at lunch-time. People were avoiding him. In fact, the only time anyone made contact with him at all was to ask him to do things for them.

Session Two

*Walter learns the true nature of assertiveness,
boundaries and expectations*

"It's not working," cried Walter, storming into the office and slumping dramatically down onto the chair. "Now people are just sending emails and leaving notes for me without talking to me. Everyone is avoiding me. They stop talking whenever I enter a room."

The Doctor raised his eyebrows in wonderment and asked: "Why do you think people are doing that?"

"Because I took your advice!" exclaimed Walter. "And set some boundaries... and told them 'NO!'"

"Ah!" intoned the Doctor, realising that Walter had gone far beyond making a note of how his time was being used... indeed, it appeared that Walter had *really* taken matters into his own hands. "Okay, so you seem to have mastered one side of assertiveness. Now let's explore the other side. You found your voice and you expressed yourself. However, perhaps this was done without thinking about the people you were dealing with... I assume that maintaining relationships is still important to you?"

"Of course," said Walter, still wanting it to be someone else's fault. "But you said I had to stand up for myself!"

"Oh dear indeed," said the Doctor, seeing that Walter had taken one half of a story and made a whole. "How about standing up for yourself in such a way that it takes other people's feelings into consideration too? True assertiveness is the synthesis of 'expression' and 'empathy'. It seems as if you may have flipped from 'passive' behaviour to 'aggressive' behaviour. A few weeks ago you were so empathetic to other people's needs that you didn't take your own needs into account. Now you are expressing your own needs so strongly you are forgetting to empathise with others."

"I... well..." Walter spluttered. "Help!"

"Your next step will be to find the balance between the two," said the Doctor taking a piece of paper and jotting down a diagram. "Let me show you:

	Aggressive	Assertive
High	Expressing one's own needs and opinions without appearing to care for the needs and opinions of others.	Being prepared to express one's own needs and opinions whilst respecting the needs and opinions of others.
	Passive-Aggressive	Passive
Low	Unable or unwilling to express one's own needs and opinions whilst disrespecting the needs and opinions of others.	Being so concerned for other's needs and opinions that one's own needs and opinions go unexpressed.

Expression

Low   High

Empathy

Walter stared at the quadrant for a few moments. "Are you saying I'm aggressive?"

"Hmm," hemmed the Doctor, considering how to continue with grace. "I'm suggesting that you have been using more aggressive behaviours than you used to and that it may have confused people. Imagine that someone gives you a lift home each day and appears happy to do so. Suddenly, one afternoon they shout at you that they are not going to give you a lift anymore. Wouldn't you wonder what had happened?"

"Oh my!" exclaimed Walter, realisation dawning.

"It's making sense?" asked the Doctor tentatively.

"Yes..." moaned Walter, thinking of how rude he had been to his colleagues. "How can I be assertive then?"

"Well, let's recap on the last session," suggested the Doctor. "As well as people using your time inappropriately... or taking advantage of you, there *are* some tasks that people might reasonably ask for your help with. These things are connected with your job role and help you achieve the purpose of your job."

"Yes," agreed Walter. "So those are the things I should be empathetic about?"

"Well, yes, though you can still be empathetic when someone asks you to do something that is really their job."

"How?"

"You might say something like: 'I get that you need this doing soon, but I'm afraid it's not something I can help you with today.'"

"Ooh. That's good!" nodded Walter, getting out his pen and writing down some notes. "Have you got any others?"

"Of course!" laughed the Doctor. "What you need to remember when saying 'no' is that you are actually attempting to *maintain your boundaries* and *manage expectations*. If you don't respect your boundaries, other people will, often unintentionally, continue to ignore them as well."

"Seems to me... that in order to maintain my boundaries, I need to know what they are first. How do I know what my boundaries are?"

"Okay," considered the Doctor. "Ask yourself:

If they weren't asking me to do that, what would I be doing instead?

"Hence, what will saying 'no' allow you to do in this situation? What part of your job *could* you be getting on with? This may be your boundary... i.e. the thing you need to get done for yourself. Then the question becomes:

Can you maintain your boundary and
help the other person in some way?"

"What a thought," chuckled Walter. "Helping others *and* getting my job done!"

"Before you say 'yes' or 'no' to someone, it is usually worth finding out a bit more information about what they need from you. Then, if necessary, ask for time to think about it. Whilst you may not be able to help them with everything, can you agree to part of what they are looking for?"

"And if they really *do* want me to do everything?" asked Walter.

"Find out *why* they want it," replied the Doctor. "What do they want it for? Ask them what they ultimately want to achieve. In other words... they want you to do this task in order to what? Can you help them with their ultimate goal in another way that is *easier for you*?"

"And what if it's not actually my job to do all of that?"

"Then find some other ways of saying 'no'!" The Doctor responded. "If you'd like some options, here are six approaches to saying 'no'. These will give you ways of maintaining your boundaries without always giving an outright 'no'!" Once again, the Doctor drew a diagram and handed it to Walter:

THE SIX 'NO'S

Compromising No

I can't stay till 6.00 but I could stay till 5.30. Perhaps we can get someone else to help too.

The point here is to give something but still maintain your boundaries.

Problem Solving No

I'm not in a position to help you... Have you checked the manual?

Offer an alternative solution that stops it from becoming your problem.

Postponing No

I can't do that now, but I could help you later.

Make sure that you keep your promise if they ask you to help later!

Negotiating No

If you can help me with this, then I can help you with that.

Here you are offering to 'exchange' tasks.

Closing No

I understand this is important for you but 'no', I'm not in a position to do that.

This is a definite no where you want to close the conversation down.

Reprioritising No

I'm happy to do that, but something else has got to give. What would you suggest?

Particularly good with management! You are demonstrating willingness whilst pointing out that you have a busy schedule.

Walter and the Doctor considered the six 'no's for a moment. "With the problem solving 'no'", the Doctor added, "it's important not to take on the role of *having* to solve the problem for them. Otherwise, that may become a whole new task in itself."

"That's true," said Walter. "My neighbour had a friend who needed someone to look after their cat whilst they were on holiday. My neighbour said that they couldn't do it themselves but would try to find someone else who could. I guess they felt like they were letting their friend down. They then spent ages finding accommodation for their friend's cat!"

"What a marvellous example," smiled the Doctor. "I might put that in my book!"

As Walter continued to read through the Six 'No's, he wondered out loud: "What if I've always helped them before? It seems mean somehow if I suddenly start saying 'no'."

"If you want to warn them of your impending 'no' then tell them you will help them this time but from now on they will need to do it themselves... or get someone else to help them. Then, if they come back next time, remind them that you both agreed they would do it themselves from now on. It is important to stick to your 'no' on the second occasion, otherwise you'll lose credibility."

"Okay," said Walter after some reflection time. "You mentioned earlier about saying you need time to think about it. I know some people that would pressure me into giving them an answer there and then."

"Well, if they are genuinely pushy to the point of being aggressive, you might give them the hard-line approach. Tell them that if they need an answer now, the answer is 'no'... or they can give you time to think about it."

"Ooh... that's a bit brutal," said Walter, wincing a little.

"It's not something you would use very often, that's for sure!" agreed the Doctor. "Another way of looking at managing boundaries is what I call the 'Scope Box'. This is designed to generate a bunch of ideas on how to contain 'incoming' activities."

"Scope Box?" queried Walter. "Sounds like the thing people stand on when they want to have a rant!"

"Ahh... No!" said the Doctor. "The 'scope' is 'that which is defined as relevant or not'. If something is within the scope then it will be covered. If something is outside the scope then it is not part of what I can do. For example, if I'm running a project, I need to know the scope of the project... what it is designed to do... what it will cover and what it will therefore not cover. If someone wants the project to deliver something else, that thing may be outside the scope and hence require a separate project."

"That's like meetings and presentations," Walter added. "You set an agenda and then that's the scope. If people want to talk about something not on the agenda, then it may be outside the scope of the meeting."

"Good, yes," agreed the Doctor. "So from a time management perspective, your scope is your agenda for the day or week. The 'Scope Box' is the time you have available to do what you need to get done. The edges of the box are your boundaries. If someone wants to add something to your day, how does that fit into your Scope Box?"

The Doctor drew a simple box with an arrow leading into it.

"When we visualise it like this," said the Doctor. "We can then visualise ideas as to how we might contain the incoming task. Most of these ideas allow you to maintain your boundary whilst still helping the other person if you can. Remember that your boundary is what you would have got done otherwise."

"Show me!" said Walter, leaning forward to look at what the Doctor was writing.

"Remember, you have a set amount of time in which to achieve your outcome, i.e. to deliver on your job role. There is unlikely to be enough time to do everything, so the challenge is deciding what to do with new requests that come in… particularly when you have already defined the scope of your day or week."

"Or meeting or presentation or project," added Walter.

"Indeed," said the Doctor. "Here are some generic ideas:"

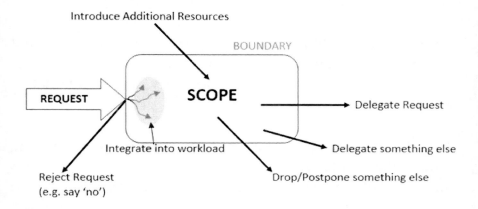

"Okay," said Walter, keen to explore some more ideas. "This seems to link to the ways of saying 'no' without saying 'no'... that we covered earlier on. So let me see if there are some more ideas for handling the requests."

Walter took the Doctor's pen and wrote underneath the diagram:

- Reject part of the task and accept part
- Problem solve their request/goal in another way
- Problem solve your own workload to make time
- Help them do it themselves (e.g. train them)
- Refer it to someone else
- Defer it to another time
- Swap request for something else you

would have done otherwise

"Excellent," said the Doctor. "Now you're getting it!"

"And the best solution would depend on the context," said Walter, thinking out loud. "It might depend on who is asking, what time of day it is, how open they are to alternative ideas…"

"Good… now… before we finish, beware of people saying things like 'could you do this for me, it will only take a minute'. They rarely mean a minute. The same is true for 'have you got a moment?' One way of handling this approach is to say: 'If it really is a minute… otherwise I'll need to schedule some time in later on.'"

"I do get a lot of interruptions," sighed Walter. "It's very annoying."

"So we'll return to handling interruptions next time!" said the Doctor, a warm smile lighting up his face. "Until then… good luck!"

Walter's Notes

Assertiveness is a combination of 'Expression' and 'Empathy' – Being able to say what I need whilst taking other people's needs into consideration.

Saying 'no' is really about maintaining my boundaries and managing other people's expectations.

If someone asks me to do something: What would I be doing if I wasn't doing that? If this is my boundary (i.e. to still get my task achieved), can I maintain my boundary whilst still helping them in some way... and not just saying no?

There are six (or more) ways of saying 'no'... and five of them don't involve saying 'no'!!

1. Defer it to later
2. Compromise and perhaps help them with part of it
3. Reprioritise my work so I can fit it in whilst pushing something else to a later date
4. Negotiate! If they do something for me, I can do something for them!

5. Problem solve to give them an alternative solution that doesn't require my time.

'Have you got a minute' or 'it will only take a minute' rarely means a minute!

Second Slice

Who Stole My Pie

A Third Slice of Pie

Who Stole My Pie

Walter's pie problems were beginning to ease.

After his session with the Doctor, Walter was getting the swing of understanding and setting boundaries.

He had asked himself: "With regards to my pies, what do I actually want or need?" He then answered with: "To have enough pie to feel full". This, he realised was his boundary.

He also realised that this would probably change from day to day. Some days there might be some pie left over and other days not.

This led to him deciding that he would share what he didn't want that day.

Life became a little easier. When someone asked him: "Can I have some of your pie?" he would reply: "If I have any pie left over, you are welcome."

The only drawback was the amount of people hanging around his desk at lunchtime watching him eat his pie. There were so many hopeful faces that it was becoming awkward to decide who should have the remaining slices. Some people were being extra nice to him and talking to him about interesting things... all in a bid to curry favour.

Whilst it was nice that people were being so friendly, it seemed that his pies were becoming a curse again instead of a pleasure. Whoever he gave the pie too, he felt guilty not giving it to others. He was almost tempted to once again bring in two pies each day.

He wanted to sort this out but he didn't know how. He'd been so clever with his boundaries, but now it was all going wrong again.

Session Three

Walter learns how his time is being used and how he could gain more control of it

As was the developing pattern at the start of each session so far, Walter was ranting again: "I can't get on with my job! People keep interrupting me and hanging round my desk. It's nice that people are talking to me again but I have to keep stopping there and then to talk to them... Even if it is a quick conversation, it takes me out of what I'm doing. Then, yesterday, the system was down for a while. It's like everything is conspiring against me to stop me doing my job."

"Sounds like your environment is making you quite reactive at the moment," empathised the Doctor.

"You're not kidding!"

"Okay, so would it be useful to look at ways of becoming less reactive?"

"We can look at it all you like," snorted Walter. "But I don't think it will help in the real world!"

The Doctor smiled. "Are you familiar with 'proactive' and 'reactive'?"

"I think so..." Walter considered. "Proactive is getting ahead of the game and doing things I intended to do... In other words all the things I'm trying to do but can't because reactive stuff keeps happening that I have no control over."

"That's it!" exclaimed the Doctor in an oddly excited fashion. "Just out of curiosity, on average what percentage of your time is spent proactively versus reactively at the moment?"

"Probably about 25% proactive and 75% reactive," Walter answered. "It used to be better than that… Now I never seem to get through my to-do list… In fact some days I don't seem to get anywhere near starting on it."

"It's interesting isn't it," announced the Doctor. "That we get into a mind-set of 'proactive is good' and 'reactive is bad'."

"But it's true," said Walter. "I hate being reactive!"

"Fair enough," said the Doctor. "But some jobs are very reactive by their nature. For example, a receptionist's job is very reactive. They don't know when people are going to call or pop in. But does that mean their job is bad? Of course not!"

"But they know that their time will work that way," Walter said, then added: "A friend of mine works at a service desk and he likes it because he never knows what's coming next!"

"So the difference is," began the Doctor, "people who enjoy that kind of job usually have a system of some sort which helps them do what they do. They know what they can deal with themselves and who else to put calls through to. In a chaotic environment, they still seem to be organised! Whilst they cannot be proactive, they do appear to be 'responsive'. So how about we make a distinction between 'reactive' and 'responsive'?"

"So reactive is like a knee-jerk reaction... almost without thought whilst responsive implies some thinking process going on?"

"Precisely... that's it!" said the Doctor. "It's a bit of a cliché now, but when we act in response, we take 'response-ability' for our actions. To be reactive tends to be out of control and consistently surprised by the unexpected. To be responsive means having systems in place for handling the unexpected."

"Aren't the *things that happen* the reactive part? It seems to me that my desk has become a reactive environment and so I get reactive as a result of it."

"To some extent, yes," agreed the Doctor. "We can look at it both ways... *reactive events* happen to you and are not initiated by you. They are usually unpredictable and often outside your control. *Being reactive* means having ineffective and usually inefficient strategies for handling people and activities."

"But are you saying that you can be in a reactive environment but still be responsive?" queried Walter, an eyebrow raising incredulously.

"That's right!" agreed the Doctor. "And it goes further! So far we have only really been talking about things that impact on you. We haven't talked about the things that you are in control of... the things that are on your to-do list."

"The stuff I never seem to get to!"

"So it seems!" smiled the Doctor. "Steven Covey[1] made a neat distinction between 'you acting on things' and 'things acting on you'. With this in mind, the next question needs to be 'how effectively do you handle those things?' We can be reactive or responsive to the things that *act on us*, but we can be proactive or inactive with the things *we act on*. So... proactive is effective and inactive is ineffective."

"I know that proactive means being planned and organised and getting things done that are on my to-do list. But what do you mean 'inactive'?"

"Inactive means not getting on with it!" the Doctor exclaimed. "To be inactive is to procrastinate... to put things off and delay them... sometimes until they become urgent. Then they tend to become reactive, where people are interrupting you and asking for it. Everything becomes chaotic again."

"That happens to me a lot," sighed Walter. "I have things I know I need to do, but I don't get round to doing them and then other people go nuts. Usually the same people that have been interrupting me and preventing me from doing the thing they really want me to do!"

The Doctor scribbled some ideas onto a pad. "Here's a model that puts these ideas together..."

TASK MANAGEMENT

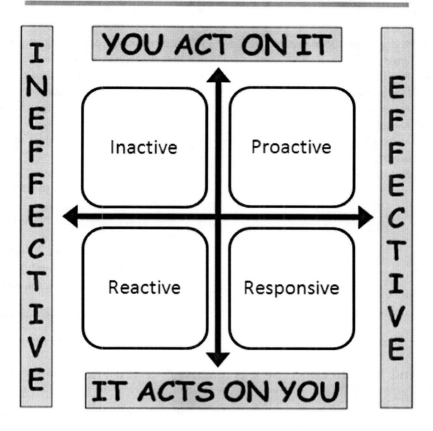

"Makes sense, but how does it help practically?" asked Walter.

"Well let's start with how to become less reactive and more responsive. First, ask yourself...

What are some of my reactive tasks and what makes me reactive?"

The Doctor then drew two columns and explained it to Walter as he wrote:

Internal Influences	External Influences
Personality style can create/ maintain reactive behaviour, e.g.: • Trying to do too many things at once • Panicking • Not being assertive • Attempting to do it all yourself • Taking too long over tasks • Making mistakes by doing tasks too quickly • Not taking time to plan	• Sudden schedule or priority changes • Interruptions from team members (those you manage) • Interruptions from managers (those that manage you) • Interruptions from colleagues • Interruptions from customers • People and tasks taking up more time than expected • Incoming emails and phone calls • Equipment failure • Taking on a new urgent task (e.g. that has been delegated to you) • Mistakes • Covering for others (e.g. not turning up) • Delays, having to wait for others • "Critical Unforeseen Events" (e.g. bad weather, traffic jams, moving goalposts) • People not doing what you ask (or not doing it correctly)

"And how do I become less reactive?" asked Walter.

"Okay, here are some ideas," said the Doctor. "Firstly, **remove yourself from the reactive events**. Can you go somewhere for an hour to get an hour's work done? A place free from interruptions... perhaps a meeting room, the corner of the restaurant or a morning working from home. If you are part of a team, can the team cover you for a bit and then you cover for them later... set up a kind of rota system of cover? If you take a time-out, treat it like a meeting or appointment so that colleagues would only interrupt you if they would interrupt you in a meeting."

"A meeting with myself," laughed Walter. "I like that idea... though it sounds a bit weird. 'I have an appointment with myself!' I guess I wouldn't say that out loud! Maybe I could send myself a meeting invitation!"

"But make sure you don't then decline the invitation because you're too busy," smiled the Doctor.

"Actually, booking time out on the system as if I'm in a meeting is not such a bad idea," considered Walter. "It would stop other people booking my time out without asking me. Anyhow, what's the next idea?"

"Secondly," continued the Doctor. "**Remove reactive events from yourself**. If you can, put your phone on temporary voice-mail or divert it to a colleague's phone... with their permission of course. Then pick up your messages and add them to your to-do list. Here's the big one... switch off the automatic flag-up system on your emails. Then, pick up your emails *when you choose* to. Schedule this into your day."

"That's a good idea," said Walter. "I guess otherwise emails act like the phone ringing... you tend to try and deal with it there and then. By the way, I've often wondered what would happen if you diverted your phone to someone else's and then they diverted their phone to yours. What would happen if someone called in? Would they get sucked into a voicemail vortex?"

"Perhaps you could try it..." the Doctor whispered conspiratorially. "But don't say I said so!" His voice raised again as he continued his advice. "Now, the third idea is the one you've been waiting for... **manage interruptions**! First and foremost, keep interruptions short and sweet! Stick to the point and put a time limit on it if possible. Reschedule the interruption to later. If it's a social... talk at lunchtime. If it requires a proper discussion, then set a specific time aside later. Let people know when your quieter times are, for example between 4.00 and 5.00. That way you can schedule interruptions into a specific time period. Finally, if you know someone is going to interrupt you at some random point during the day, visit or phone the interrupter before they come to you. That way it can fit *your* schedule... and it is much easier to leave someone else's desk than it is to get them to leave yours!"

"I've had parties like that," smiled Walter nostalgically. "Always better to go to someone else's party... then you can leave when you want to! Okay, so you mentioned getting more proactive and less inactive. What was that about?"

"Being inactive is usually about procrastination," explained the Doctor.

"Oooh!" exclaimed Walter. "We could call that 'procrastinative'!"

"That's not really a word," said the Doctor.

"It is now!" announced Walter cheerfully.

"Yes well, I suppose it's no worse that some of the other management jargon we invent," said the Doctor thoughtfully. "Anyway, we digress."

"Or are we being procrastinative?" asked Walter.

"Quite," said the Doctor. "So, inactive... or *procrastinative* means putting things off instead of getting them done. It often means doing less essential tasks instead of the one we need to be doing. Then the thing we need to be doing ends up getting more and more urgent and pressing. This can be bad news for others if they are relying on you getting that thing done on time."

"Sometimes I get more motivation if I leave it to the last minute!"

"That's okay if you still do a good job and meet the deadline," nodded the Doctor. "Then be honest with yourself that you *are* going to do it at the last minute, schedule it in your diary and then, if necessary, let others know when you are going to do it. The issue behind procrastination is the feeling that you 'ought' to be doing it when you are doing other things. I know someone who used to have a list of things they *should* do and a list of things they *wanted* to do. They worked on the principle that they would get the 'should' list done first and then they could enjoy doing the 'want' list. However the 'should' list got longer and they ended up resenting the 'should' list and not doing that either. So for a while they were getting nothing done at all!"

"So why do people procrastinate?" asked Walter.

"Think about it for a moment," the Doctor invited. "Why do *you* sometimes put things off?" But before Walter could answer, the Doctor was scribbling on paper again. "Do any of these sound familiar?"

Why People Put Things Off... Reasons for Procrastination

Lack of Confidence
- Fear of not doing the job right/well enough, or of failing.
- Feeling uncertain, confidence has been knocked, thinking: "I can't do it".
- No-one to ask, others are busy, don't want to ask, don't want to appear stupid.

Lack of Understanding
- Unclear of the task, don't understand it, don't have enough details/facts.
- Unclear of the process, don't know where to start.
- The task is too vague/broad, not clearly defined.

Lack of Perspective
- The task is overwhelming... too big and daunting. Perhaps overly complex?

Lack of Motivation
- Don't see why it needs doing, don't see the point or don't see how it fits in.
- Don't like doing the task e.g. it's unpleasant or it's boring.
- The task is unrewarding and has little perceived benefit.
- There is no deadline... it's easy to procrastinate.

"A few of those sound familiar!" chuckled Walter. "How about 'Lack of Time'? That's the reason I usually don't get round to things."

"We will return to the 'not enough time' issue later," the Doctor instructed. "But the short answer is: 'There will always be a *lack of time* to get everything done!' It becomes a matter of choosing what you intend to do and hence acknowledge what you will probably *not* do. Then, if necessary, let affected parties know!"

"So what about the reasons for procrastinating that you've written here," asked Walter. "What can I do about them?"

"How about these?" said the Doctor and he was off again with pen and paper:

Resolving Procrastination

Confidence
- Reboost your confidence by reminding yourself of what you *can* do.
- Ask yourself: "what would *really* happen if I did make a mistake?"
- Ask for help or ask for training

Understanding
- Establish which bit you don't understand and then find out!
- Model other people who do the task effectively.

Perspective
- Write it down. Break it down into manageable/doable actions. Decide to do a bit at a time.

Motivation
- Establish why the task needs doing and how it fits in or helps. If it seems to serve no purpose ask 'where does the outcome/output of this task go when I've done it?'
- Do it at the start of the day, so you don't have to worry about it. It will be a weight off your mind, a relief!
- Reward yourself for completing the task (e.g. with a treat). Or do something you like doing after the hard task.

"Thank you," said Walter simply.

"So would you like to be more proactive?" urged the Doctor. "Would you like to get ahead of the game and become more future focussed? Do you want to plan what you do and focus on what *is* important?"

"How can I say 'no'?" laughed Walter.

"Well, I thought we dealt with that in the last session," joked the Doctor. "But I get what you mean. What we are talking about here is the first stage of getting more organised and hence feeling a greater sense of control. For this session we'll cover some ideas for combating procrastination and becoming more proactive. Next time we'll explore how to get organised with your to-do list."

"Ooh, that would be good," nodded Walter enthusiastically. "I have a rather wild and untameable to-do list. It's like a hydra, when I chop one head off, two more grow in its place. Sometimes I daren't look at it in case it attacks me."

"Well, tune in next time for 'hydra management' then!" laughed the Doctor. "For now let's get started on proactivity. The first thing is to **get a grip on the task**. If it seems too big then break it down in to component parts. This will help you figure out which bits can be done easily and which bits will need further research or breaking down into further manageable actions. If you need motivation, take yourself forward in time to the point where you have completed the task and you feel good. Whilst feeling good, ask yourself: 'What is the next smallest step I can take towards my goal?' Then it doesn't feel difficult, it feels easy!²"

"Can you give me an example?" asked Walter.

"Sure," said the Doctor. "When writing a book, the idea of 'write a book' is too big and overwhelming. Years ago I started writing a whole bunch of books and never got far. I got lost in the enormity of it all. Now, if I need inspiration, I imagine the book complete and on the bookshelf with all the other authors I admire. This gives me a buzz, so as I'm feeling the buzz I ask myself: 'What's the next smallest step?' It might be a few hundred words, it might be a few pages, but it all adds up over time."

"Are you writing a book now?" asked Walter, intrigued.

"Indeed."

"Cool. What's it about?"

"Well, it's about a chap who isn't managing his time very well and how he learns to get himself organised," responded the Doctor with an air of distractedness. Then he broke from his reverie and continued: "But we digress! Whilst it is of course important to plan your work, it is also important to spend an *appropriate* amount of time planning. If a piece of work is big, for example a project, or is particularly critical to your job role, then get to a point where you can follow the steps of your plan confidently in achieving that work. Avoid spending so much time planning however, that you don't have time to do the task itself!"

"I used to do that with exam revision timetables when I was at school," smiled Walter. "I had it all colour coded and everything. I guess it was really an avoidance strategy! Wow... weird thought that over-planning might actually be a form of procrastination!"

"So then it becomes useful to set a time and quality boundary on the work," said the Doctor. "When do you want to get the thing done by and hence how long do you have to do each part? Then, particularly if you are a perfectionist, ask yourself 'What is realistically good enough? How detailed does it *really* need to be?' Avoid spending hours on things that only need to take a few minutes. Avoid producing a thirty page document when all that was required was a one page overview."

"Yes, of course," nodded Walter in total agreement.

"Here's another thing to consider," said the Doctor. "Is there a template, model or exemplar that you can work to?"

"Exemplar?" asked Walter.

"An example of 'best practice'," replied the Doctor.

"That would be nice!" Walter concurred. "I guess I could create my own templates."

"Okay," continued the Doctor. "Now another way to be proactive is to **make use of 'dead time'**!"

"You what now? Dead time?" asked Walter. "I assume you are not referring to Zombies and the like?"

"Ah, no," smiled the Doctor. "It's where you don't seem to be able to do anything productive due to external circumstances. A classic example might be waiting for someone or something. If you take a few small things with you to do, it's amazing how much you can get done by making use of that time. It might also be an opportunity to come up with ideas. All you need to do is focus your brain on something. If you sit there getting bored, your brain will tend to run off on its own course. Another use of dead time is listening to audio books whilst in the car. That way you can either be educated or entertained as you sit in traffic! I've listened to some classic books that I never would have had time to read."

"What a novel idea," said Walter. "Like listening to what Bertie Wooster[3] called 'an improving book'!"

"Sweet!" said the Doctor. "Alternatively, you might use that time to relax for a while... to empty your mind and chill out."

"Ah... relaxation... I think I remember that."

"The final thing for now is to make decisions," said the Doctor. "This is another area where some people struggle; perhaps because they feel they don't have enough information, or maybe they have *too much* information. Sometimes it may be because of the perceived consequences. The problem here is that an unmade decision may become stressful for the individual and troublesome for others in the organisation. Of course, decision making could fill a whole book but here's the 'skinny' version:"

The Quick Guide to Decision Making

1) Write down the options.

2) For each option write down the pros and cons (to you personally or the team or the business etc. depending on the context of the decision).

3) Score each of the pros 1-5 where 1 is relatively low importance through to 5 which is essential. Then do the same for the cons, where 1 is not really an issue and 5 is a serious consideration. Does one option stand out as being most advantageous? Could you prevent and/or handle the cons of this option as if they are risks? If possible, does it make sense to have a plan 'a' and a plan 'b'?

4) If it is still too close to call or you'd like a 'best of all worlds' solution, look at the pros for *all* options collectively, particularly the 4s and 5s. Now treat these as a list of requirements. Looking at a unified list of requirements, what solution (or set of solutions) might give you *all* of those things? When you have a new idea, you can then check for any risks of this idea and plan how to mitigate or handle those risks.

5) Communicate your decision to all who need to know. Then take action.

"I'm normally pretty good at making decisions," said Walter. "But that's useful because I tend not to write things down. Then if I'm challenged I don't really have a leg to stand on. If I write it down and score it, I can justify my decision if I need to."

"Excellent!" the Doctor exclaimed. "Well I think that does it for this session. Next time, bring your to-do list!"

Walter's Notes

Being responsive means using the past to inform the future. If something makes me reactive, what can I learn from this? ... "If that happens again, I will..."

To be truly responsive means allocating time to reviewing how things are working and then exploring efficiencies and solutions to common faults and issues. It may mean putting in new processes to prevent issues from occurring. In this sense, responsive becomes proactive.

In order to become more responsive, I need to:

    a) Move myself away from reactive tasks/environments
    b) Move reactive tasks away from me
    c) Handle interruptions more effectively...

THEN I can get more work done!

AND THEN... I need to stop procrastinating and get things done before they get too close to the deadline.

I CAN do this by being pro-active:

a) Get a grip on the task – break it down and ask questions about any bits I don't understand.
b) Make better use of 'dead-time' (e.g. when I'm waiting for things)
c) Make decisions… before they get made for me!

Third Slice

Who Stole My Pie

A Fourth Slice of Pie

Who Stole My Pie

Demand for pie was still outweighing supply, and Walter was experiencing two pie related problems.

Firstly, some of the team were accusing Walter of favouritism. They felt that others were getting more pie than they were. "It's not fair" They would say. Indeed, some of Walter's colleagues had been trying to bribe Walter with offers of chocolates and sweets. Other colleagues were resorting to emotional blackmail: "And after all the things I've done for you... and you give the pie to someone else!"

The second problem was the amount of people watching him eat his pie. Sometimes, Walter felt like he was in a zoo as the main attraction: "Oooh look... It's feeding time at Walter's desk... Let's all stand round and watch him!" Lunchtime was not a pleasant experience and he was really not enjoying his pie anymore. He was almost considering bringing in sandwiches and forgetting the whole pie ordeal.

So Walter stopped and thought for a bit. Then he decided upon a two pronged solution.

The first part of the solution was to set up a 'pie-chart', which was, in effect, a rota. If people wanted pie, they put themselves on a list and then their name was added to the rotating pie-chart. In addition, Walter set time aside for pie related requests. If people wanted to talk pie, they knew when to visit him. This also enabled Walter to defer any random pie-talk to that time.

Who Stole My Pie

The other prong was for Walter to eat his pie away from his desk (or 'the monkey cage' as he had come to think of it). He tried a corner of the canteen but was asked not to bring his own food. So he found a spot outside to sit, which was rather pleasant on a sunny day. On rainy days however, he retreated to his car to eat his pie uninterrupted.

This 'desk-escape' plan was not totally satisfactory to Walter and was becoming a bit of hassle. However, it seemed the best compromise he could think of.

Session Four

Walter learns about prioritising

"Good to see you again," smiled the Doctor. "How are you doing?"

"Well," began Walter, "I'm endeavouring to take more action... and sometimes I can get ahead of the game. I think I'm less reactive than before too. I've been making some templates and other people have also found them useful. I've managed to sneak off a few times to get some work done in a meeting room... and I've switched my email alert off though I'm probably still checking them too often! I think I am making better decisions and my manager was pleased when I showed him how and why I was making decisions now... you know, by writing them down."

"That's great!" said the Doctor.

"The problem is I can't get to the bottom of my to-do list! I've got the teeth of the hydra upon me!"

"Well bang a gong!" the Doctor grinned. "Okay, let's start with a stark reality here...

Who Stole My Pie

There will never be enough time to do everything on the to-do list."

"Oh man!" said Walter, his shoulders slumping. "I thought that was true for us mere mortals... but even for you? I was hoping for a few tips and techniques to get absolutely everything done!"

"Well how about this session we explore the difference between *fantasy* and *reality* time management?" suggested the Doctor. "We can start with something you said just now: You are becoming less reactive. That's great news! A while ago you said your average time control percentage was about 25% proactive and 75% reactive. So for everything you had planned to do, there was always going to be a bunch of other things that would land on your desk?"

"That's right," Walter agreed. "I think it's a bit better now... maybe 50% proactive and 50% reactive."

"That's certainly an improvement!" encouraged the Doctor. "This 'time control' percentage is going to prove to be at the very core of you organising yourself. Believe it or not, it will become a magic formula that you can run everything through from now on!"

"I might call it the 'RePro' percentage!" announced Walter.

"Nice! I like it!" exclaimed the Doctor. "Okay, so is it fair to say that for every task you plan to do, there will often be other things that crop up... and then this makes the task take longer than expected?"

"Yes," answered Walter with a single definite nod.

"So this means we have a 'fantasy-reality gap' between *what you think you ought to get done* versus *what actually gets done*. Consider this: if your job is 50% proactive and hence 50% reactive... how long will it take you to get an hour of planned work done... on average?"

"I guess it will take about two hours," Walter concluded. "So in my case I'll only get done half of what I expect to get done! Good grief!"

"Yes," agreed the Doctor. "For some reason we get very optimistic with how long we think things will take... and hence what we think we will achieve. I'm not suggesting we should be pessimistic... but rather *realistic*. Most people underestimate how long things will take."

"That's so true," said Walter, nodding vigorously.

"The reason is that the reactive stuff is 'unknown' and intangible. We can't write down *what* will happen or *when* it will happen because it is unpredictable. In this sense, we find it hard to block out time for 'invisible' potential tasks. Just to give you an idea, here's how long an hour's task will take depending on your proactive percentage[1]:"

Proactive %	Reactive %	1 Hours planned work will take...
100%	0%	1 Hour
90%	10%	1 Hour 7 Mins
80%	20%	1 Hour 15 Mins
75%	25%	1 Hour 20 Mins
70%	30%	1 Hour 26 Mins
60%	40%	1 Hour 40 Mins
50%	50%	2 Hours
40%	60%	2 Hours 30 Mins
30%	70%	3 Hours 20 Mins
25%	75%	4 Hours
20%	80%	5 Hours
10%	90%	10 Hours

"So," continued the Doctor. "Now you *know* that every task will take longer than expected... whenever you say yes to a task, add a percentage of time depending on your average 'RePro' percentage. For you, if you are in the environment where reactive stuff happens, it will take two hours to get an hour's work done. For every task you say 'yes' to, remember to double the time you think it will take… and that will help to account for the reactive stuff!"

"Crikey!" exclaimed Walter. "That's pretty scary but it makes sense. I used to be about 25% proactive and it did take about four hours to get an hour's work done. Now it probably *does* take a couple of hours. Wow. No wonder I'm getting more done! And that's a really useful idea... when someone asks me to do something for them: run it through the formula and that's how much time it will really take me!"

"Hopefully, the percentage gives you the 'worst case scenario'," said the Doctor. "If you can then get away from your desk and emails for a bit, you can get more done."

"This is what we covered last time about reducing the reactive tasks and events," Walter reflected.

"Yes," said the Doctor. "And does this also help you to link back to *managing boundaries and expectations*? If you're sitting in a meeting and someone says: 'can you do this', instead of thinking 'that'll only take an hour', you know it will take you twice that. Consider how you used to be: an hour's work you took on would take four hours to complete. That's more than half a day! Considering you only have 10 half days in a week, you would have just lost a tenth of it!"

"We really do get overly optimistic about what we can achieve and how long things will take!" considered Walter. "Okay... do you have any more 'reality time management' for me?"

"Of course!" laughed the Doctor. "When you get good at this, your plans for the day and week will pretty much reflect what you *actually* get done. So let's look at the practical centre-point of your time management... the 'to-do' list."

"Ah yes," Walter winced. "The dreaded hydra!"

"When do you write or update your to-do list?" asked the Doctor.

"Well, I used to write it in the morning when I first got in to the office... but I found that I would often get interrupted immediately... and *then I wasn't even planning my day!* It started randomly and continued that way. I didn't really know if I was being productive or not! Nowadays I tend to keep one list and I add to it as the need arises."

"And how does that work for you?" the Doctor enquired.

"Generally okay," Walter responded. "Although some things disappear off the top of the page from time to time and get forgotten about... particularly when I'm extra busy."

"Well here's a recommendation for you," said the Doctor. "Update it just before you go home at the end of the day. That way it's still fresh in your mind and you don't have to mentally take it home with you. Some people find themselves waking up in the middle of the night rehearsing their to-do list to make sure they remember it the next day!"

"Oh yes, I've had that experience!" said Walter. "I guess in my job it would be easier to find a few minutes at the end of the day than it would be at the start. It also means I'm ready to take on the day... already prepared!"

"Now," said the Doctor, leaning forward as if to make a serious point. "The other thing you might want to check from time to time is *where do these things come from* that end up on your to-do list? For example, do they come from your own job role and objectives? Delegated tasks from your manager? Projects? Enquiries from colleagues and customers that are related to your job? Or do they come from the 'being helpful' tasks that you do for other colleagues? It is a good idea to check these from time to time to make sure the balance is working for you and that you are actually fulfilling the purpose of your job role!"

"That's true," agreed Walter. "I don't tend to think of things in that way. I just do what needs to be done... which could come from anywhere!"

"Some people organise themselves by having a 'Master To-Do List'," said the Doctor wincing a little.

"Are you alright?" asked Walter.

"Yes, fine thanks," smiled the Doctor. "Just had something in my eye. Anyway, the master list covers *everything* that you need to do. It may even have a hundred things on it! They may come from your objectives, meetings, conversations and emails. They will often link to what you have in your in-tray."

"What about projects?" asked Walter.

"Each project will have its own list of actions, but it is worth putting the title of each project on the master list too."

"Crikey," said Walter. "That would be a long list!"

"Yes, it might be," agreed the Doctor. "It depends on your job. Of course it is essential to review the master list from time to time to make sure priorities are getting done. Now, the trick is to pull about *ten* things off the master list that you want to get done and then this becomes your *active to-do list*... the things you intend to get done in the short term."

"Phew! That would certainly be less overwhelming than organising a hundred tasks!" Walter then added: "So it's a bit like having a filing-cabinet where everything in it needs to be done but you just take out a few things at a time in order to focus on them."

"Okay," said the Doctor. "So imagine you had ten things on your to-do list."

"Luxury!" said Walter, gazing dreamily at the ceiling. "I always dreamed of having just ten items on my to-do list."

"Okay... Well now you do... obviously with a bigger master to-do list in the background," smiled the Doctor. "Taking those ten things, how would you prioritise them?"

"Probably by taking the one that is shouting at me loudest!" said Walter after a moment's thought. "I mean the one with the biggest consequences."

"Well that's not a bad approach when everything is critical and urgent," said the Doctor. "However, when you look at the list *try prioritising by purpose and then timing*. Remember that prioritising is not just about *how soon* you do something but also *how long* you spend on it. If it helps you to achieve your purpose then spend the time you need on it to get it done. If it doesn't help you achieve your purpose (but perhaps it helps someone else achieve theirs), do it but spend the shortest amount of time on it to get it back to them as soon as you can! Avoid the 'perfectionist trap'... 'If I'm doing this for someone else I'd better do it properly and spend 8 hours on it!' Ask yourself: 'What is the minimum action from me that will still give them what they need?'"

"Doesn't that mean you end up rushing stuff for other people?" asked Walter, looking like he'd just been pinched. "Won't the quality suffer as a result?"

"The important thing here is to get good at nailing down their requirements when they ask you to do something for them," said the Doctor. "Make sure you have a clear idea of what they *actually need from you* before taking action. Otherwise you are in the arena of uncertainty and mindreading. Therein lie the time-monsters of fuzzy objectives and guesswork!"

"I agree it's a good idea to understand what they actually want," said Walter nodding. "It's certainly less stressful than guessing and hoping!"

"The next question you need to ask is: 'How soon does it *really* need doing?'" the Doctor said. "Check: *How urgent is urgent?* Of course, sometimes you may need to challenge others too... politely, of course! For some people everything is urgent... that's the way they live their lives. However, when you ask for more information, it often turns out that it doesn't need doing 'now'... but instead 'soon'."

"I had a manager like that once," Walter recollected. "Everything was urgent. He would write 'urgent' on all the files. I said to him one day that if everything was urgent, then urgency has lost its meaning because what was more urgent than what? He started writing 'V. Urgent' on some of them... and then on others 'Critical' and then others 'Emergency'. I think he was teasing me but at least he got the message! But I guess the big question is: What if everything *does* need doing now *and* is about my purpose?"

"Well," began the Doctor. "If you find that everything needs to be done as soon as possible and is all purposeful work then take the one that would cause the most issues if it didn't get done now and do that one first. This is not ideal, but it is a system!"

"Ah!" Walter intoned. "You mean: 'if I didn't get this done now, what would hit the fan, how much would hit the fan and what kind of a clear up job would it be afterwards?'"

"That is one way of looking at it!" said the Doctor, unsure what to do with that analogy. "Now let's return to your to-do list of ten things. You can now prioritise them. So what comes next?"

"I guess the ideal would be to put them in the diary," said Walter.

"Indeed, schedule them," said the Doctor smiling again. "Here we have the 'Utopia of time management'... to have a pretty good idea of what you *are* going to achieve that week and what you are doing that day! Whilst you don't know what reactive tasks might come your way, you should be able to predict how much proactive work you can get done in the timescale of a week."

"But how can I predict the unpredictable?" asked Walter.

"You don't need to know specifically what reactive stuff will come your way..." explained the Doctor. "You just need to know how much time to set aside for it. Hence your 'RePro' percentage. As you look at items on the to-do list, run each item through your formula and block out that much time to get it done. So for you, block out two hours to get each hour of work done."

"So... take each item and ask: 'how long will it take?' Then add the percentage," said Walter, more to himself than to the Doctor.

"Yes, you create yourself a 'time cushion' for the unexpected!" said the Doctor, pleased that the message was getting through. "Now you have *reality* time management!"

"Hmmm," hemmed Walter, suddenly troubled. "The only problem with this idea is that it looks like I'm not intending to do very much work that week!"

"Your choice! Your choice!" exclaimed the Doctor. "But perhaps it is better to be realistic. Then if you have some time left over to get extra things done... then that's a bonus! Have some additional extra things that you'd *like* to get done if you have time. At least this helps to avoid the constant daily disappointment of not getting everything achieved. *Better to manage other people's expectations than to promise what you cannot deliver because you had an unrealistic schedule."*

"Okay," Walter conceded. "So when it comes to time management, the bottom line here is 'be realistic' rather than over-optimistic!"

"Wherever possible, yes!" cried the Doctor, standing suddenly. "Marvellous. See you again."

Walter's Notes

Be realistic with my time and what I can do with it... stop being over optimistic!

There will never be enough time to do everything... and things will take longer than expected!

In order to account for 'dark matter' time (i.e. the stuff that is going to happen that I cannot yet see), I need to run it through the magic RE%PRO formula and add in 'blank time'! This will help me be more realistic with how much I can get done.

Remember... being 75% Reactive means one hour's work needs four hours booked out in the diary. If I aim for 50% being reactive, then I still need two hours for every hour's work I schedule.

The secret to being organised is:

1) Keep a to-do list and update it at the end of each day... ready to start on it the next working day.

2) Prioritise the to-do list according to my purpose/objectives (higher priority to things that help me achieve my role) and timing (how soon does it *really* need doing?). Prioritising is not just about how soon I need to do it, but also how long I need to spend on doing it.

3) Schedule it in to the diary adding the RE%PRO to each task.

The P.I.E. Check: What to do when I stop the world

As a summary, at any given moment in time, I can 'stop the world' and focus on these key areas:

P... Priorities...   What are my priorities right now?

I... Interests...   What do I need/want to get done?

E... Expectations... What can I also do for others?
                       What do they need to know?

(Interests help me understand my Boundaries... i.e. what I need to get done whilst also helping others.)

Who Stole My Pie

A Fifth Slice of Pie

Who Stole My Pie

There was never enough pie to share with everyone... and this was bothering Walter.

Fortunately, Walter's rotating pie-chart was popular with his colleagues. They agreed that it was fair and no-one in the department took bits of pie when it was not their day. All was going well... or was it?

A new issue had emerged for Walter. In setting up the pie-chart, the amount of pie going to others had become rather rigid. In order to have a rota, people needed to know which day they were getting a share. People like to plan ahead... particularly when it came to food. Three slices per day for others... and that was half a pie. Some days this was fine, but there were some days that Walter was still a little hungry and a lot resentful! The old voice was gaining volume in his mind... "But it's MY pie!!!"

Renown for the pie was growing. Word was spreading across the company. Walter's pie was becoming legend! And perhaps that's why disaster struck.

Someone from another department had sneaked in and stolen a slice of pie. There was uproar. Walter was angry and his colleagues seemed angrier. If this wasn't resolved quickly who knows what could happen. The start of a pie war?

Who Stole My Pie

Walter was beginning to think that they would need a lock for the cupboard and the fridge. However, whilst they tried to solve the problem of pie-pilfering, Walter was considering reducing the pie slice sharing to two slices a day for his colleagues. Or perhaps he might reduce the size of the slices?

Session Five

Walter learns the importance of communication

"Now that I'm organised," Walter moaned, "my manager and colleagues think I'm not pulling my weight."

The Doctor looked a little confused. "Why would they think that?"

"They think I don't have enough to do because I'm not running around stressing out like they are," explained Walter. "The problem is, we've got a bit of a competitive 'long-hours' culture in the office and I'm not prepared to join in. Someone was telling me that they regularly work 50 hours a week. Since we are only contracted to do 37.5 hours, I told them that means they are doing voluntary work for the company! They didn't see the funny side. When I go home on time I get comments like 'lightweight' and 'just doing half a day again'!"

"That must be frustrating," the Doctor empathised.

"You bet!" exclaimed Walter. "My manager gave me a poor rating at my one to one and told me I wasn't working hard enough. She seems to reward people who go to her with problems all the time. Anyone who just gets on with their job is overlooked."

The Doctor pondered for a moment, head resting on his chin and one eyebrow raised towards the ceiling. "I wonder if your manager likes staff to be visible. How about communicating with her? What if you were to let her know what you have on and what you are accomplishing? Let her know what challenges you are facing and how you propose to overcome them... or how you overcame them. Then let her know how things are going."

"But just because I'm organised, she thought I didn't have enough to do so she loaded me up with a bunch of new projects... and now I'm swamped and overloaded. I feel like I've gone round in a circle and now I'm back at square one." Walter sighed and stared at the floor.

"So letting her know what you have been doing should help with that," said the Doctor nodding as if in agreement with himself. "If you know you are getting overloaded, it's important to talk things through with her. However, before you do speak to her, make sure you carry out a reality check."

"What do you mean?" asked Walter.

"When we feel overloaded and under pressure, we often lose perspective," the Doctor explained. "Like looking through strange lenses, our experience gets distorted. Some people 'catastrophise' and talk in generalisations: 'It's all too much... nothing works... I can't do anything right'. When the *perceived pressure* seems to outweigh *perceived ability to cope* we tend to get stressed. However, our perception is not always a good reflection of reality! When we lose touch with reality we also lose *credibility*. So it *is* important that we deal with fact and evidence."

"Okay, that makes sense," agreed Walter. "What facts and evidence do you suggest I need?"

"Start by writing or printing out what you have on your to-do list," began the Doctor. "For each item, estimate how long it will take, adding in some time cushions for reactive things. Then look at when the deadlines are and then how much time you have available."

"Yes," Walter nodded. "We've spoken of this before."

"Good!" the Doctor exclaimed. "Now you have your evidence. The next step, if still necessary, is to set up a brief meeting with your manager. By setting time aside rather than randomly talking, you are demonstrating that it is important to you."

"What if your manager agrees to the meeting and then puts you off?" asked Walter.

"Be prepared to reschedule to the soonest possible time," said the Doctor. "If this happens a couple of times, you may need to create a spontaneous meeting. If, however, they are not prepared to discuss it at all... then you have a different issue which may need to be addressed in a different way."

"I know my manager gets busy but I don't think she would refuse to discuss the workload!" Walter smiled. "But out of curiosity, what could you do in that situation?"

"Well without digressing too far from the issue at hand, it would of course depend on what else was going on with the manager," considered the Doctor swiftly, talking as much to the air around him as to Walter. "It may be to see if other team members have similar issues and raise them at a team meeting, again with fact and evidence. If that doesn't work, you might need to raise it with their manager or with Personnel."

"Okay fair enough," said Walter, happy to bring the subject back to his own situation. "So what if your manager *is* reasonable and you *can* set some time aside?"

"Right," said the Doctor bringing his attention back to Walter. "So go through the to-do list and the deadlines. Be realistic rather than pessimistic... stay open to ideas and solutions. It may mean reprioritising or getting some work done in a meeting room. It may mean dropping an item or it being passed elsewhere." The Doctor drew breath. "The point is that your manager may not realise what work you have on all the time. So it's useful to keep the channels of communication open. Don't expect managers to keep track of everything! They may well be struggling with their own workload! So make it easy for them to manage you by communicating rather than disappearing behind your desk."

"I think in the past that I've got frustrated and then turned it into a rant!" realised Walter. "I can see my colleagues doing that too. I guess that all my manager hears from us is a bunch of complaints! I think it would make a difference to her if we went with facts and ideas for solutions."

"So how about we look at the team communication?" asked the Doctor. "How much do you know about what other team members are doing at the moment? How busy are they?"

"Everyone is busy!" laughed Walter, though not with joy. "At least they say they are! I think some people are genuinely doing more than others, though I sometimes wonder if I'm the only one doing any work around the place. Some people spend more time moaning than actually doing their job!"

"And do you know specifically what key activities other people have on their to-do list right now?" inquired the Doctor.

"Of course not!" said Walter shaking his head. "I have enough trouble with my own workload."

"Okay," said Doctor. "So this is a sign of a lack of communication around and across the team."

"But we *do* talk to each other," said Walter a little defensively. "Though not about our specific workload. It's all a bit general really. Having said that, we *do* communicate if we need information from one another. Not that we always get the information! Some people seem to like holding on to what they know."

"So they want to be indispensable?" the Doctor nodded.

"Probably," wondered Walter. "Some people *do* seem to think that they will be irreplaceable if they keep information to themselves!"

"Of course," continued the Doctor with a slightly pained expression. "The irony of holding back information is that they end up doing *more* work… If you're the only person who knows how to do something, you'll be the only person who ends up doing it! Sharing information can help to manage your workload."

"I never thought of it like that!" said Walter, nodding in appreciation.

"The more open you are about what to do, who to contact, where to go and how to do things, the more you will have time to develop skills that *really* make you indispensable…" smiled the Doctor before adding: "and dare I say it promotable!"

"Cool!" said Walter.

"So you said there is an exchange of *some* information," continued the Doctor. "But am I right that the team members don't really know what everyone else is working on at a given point in time?"

"That is correct," Walter agreed. "People talk about how busy they are but not specifically what they are doing. It does get a

bit like a competition sometimes... I'm busier than you... I'm more stressed than you! It's a bit like a badge that's used to impress the manager."

"Okay," said the Doctor. "Now I can't necessarily control how your manager manages but there is a really useful thing your team can do at weekly team meetings... When you become a manager I would certainly recommend it."

"Well my curiosity is piqued!" teased Walter. "What is this magical thing?"

The Doctor beamed at the banter. "Some teams have a whiteboard, virtual or real, where team names are written down the side and days of the working week across the top. This creates an empty chart. At every weekly meeting each person has a minute or so to update the rest of the team on what they have planned for the week... including key activities, meetings and priorities. This gets written up in brief on the whiteboard."

"So everyone knows what everyone else is up to!" Walter stated. "That can be a quick update too, so not overly time consuming? Then people would appreciate what others are doing."

"There is an added benefit that by knowing what others are up to, you know who to refer enquiries to," explained the Doctor. "If someone outside the team makes contact with a question, you know who is dealing with it."

"Yes, that would be more professional!" Walter agreed.

"By the way," added the Doctor, "it doesn't necessarily have to be done on a Monday. It really depends on what's most productive for the team. In organised environments you might be able to do it on Friday afternoon ready for next week. Other teams may need to use the Monday in order to get an idea of the priorities for that week... so a Tuesday or Wednesday meeting may be better!"

"I like the openness and transparency..." Walter nodded. "It helps to prevent secrecy, mistrust and misunderstandings. I guess it would also allow the team to help each other out from time to time. If someone has more on than others, the load could be shared out a little."

"Absolutely," said the Doctor. "And now you are talking about some of the qualities of a high performance team."

"Wow!" smiled Walter.

"The team meeting can also be an opportunity to share knowledge and information," added the Doctor. "For example, if someone has been on a training course, they might brief the team on key learning points and applications. In addition, the team might occasionally look at their top three 'time consumers' and problem solve them with a view to making things more efficient. This can help the team become more responsive and less reactive."

"We tried doing some problem solving before but it seemed that everything was ultimately outside of our control," said Walter. "The main causes of our time management problems were senior management decisions, company systems and the marketplace. Not a lot my team could do about that."

"I know," nodded the Doctor. "So you need to bring it back to what you *can* control and influence. When you perceive that the problem is 'out there' beyond your control and influence, a useful questions is: 'How is that a problem to us directly?' or 'How does that affect us directly?' The answer to this questions will tell you where you can solve the problem."

"But that doesn't solve the problem of poor management decisions and all that!" exclaimed Walter.

"Nope!" agreed the Doctor. "And those things are out of your control. You need to deal with the *impact* that it has on you. You might need to introduce a system or process that speeds up how you handle it. Or you might have a ground rule that if X happens, you will do Y."

"But doesn't that just create 'sticking plaster' solutions?" asked Walter. "It doesn't actually cure anything."

"If you cannot prevent the problem from happening, then look to prevent it becoming a problem for *you*," said the Doctor. "If you can't stop it then the best you can do is stop it from creating an issue for you."

"Do you mean creating a barrier or shield against the problem?"

"Or a filter," added the Doctor. "Or a funnel perhaps. Anything that prevents it from causing you additional grief. The point here is to feel like you are back in the driving seat. When we can only see the problem as 'out there' we tend to become a victim of the situation. It is better to feel empowered by taking control and figuring out what you *can* do and how you will go about it."

"Okay, so the focussed weekly meeting is a great idea!" said Walter with more enthusiasm than he would ever have granted the idea of a team meeting! "It also gives the manager an opportunity to brief the team on any updates... and get people ready for the week ahead. I'm beginning to see how essential these channels of communication are across the team as well as to and from the manager."

"In that case," said the Doctor with a single, definite nod. "I suggest we call it a day!"

Walter's Notes

1) Communicate with my manager about what I'm doing, what challenges I'm facing and how I'm dealing with them. Keep her in the loop!

   Set a brief meeting with my manager from time to time, particularly if I'm getting overloaded and/or struggling.

   Make sure what I am saying is factual and evidence based.

2) Communicate with the team to find out what they are working on and let them know what I am up to.

   Suggest using a whiteboard to update one another with our key activities.

   Share useful information that could help to make our work easier.

Who Stole My Pie

A Sixth Slice of Pie

Who Stole My Pie

Why hadn't he done this sooner?

Walter had had a revelation... a momentous realisation... "Share the information!"

And so the pie-club was born.

One morning in the pie-shop, Walter noticed a take-away menu. This gave him an idea. He asked for a few menus and the pie-shop-keeper gladly gave him some, along with a few fliers. At work, Walter made the menu available to colleagues and for the first time revealed his secret... the location of the magical, mystical pie-shop!

Soon, he set up a pie-club where everyone bought a pie and brought it in to share with other pie-club members. After a bit of trial and error (including a few people that were regularly 'forgetting' to buy a pie but still expecting a share of the pie-feast), the rules of the pie-club were formed... the Primary Pie Principle on any day being: "No Buy, No Pie!"

In addition, Walter shared details of the pie-shop with the rest of the company, posting flyers on notice boards everywhere.

Who Stole My Pie

With the information shared and the vigilance of the pie-club, there were no more cases of pie-pilfering. Indeed, some other departments created their own pie-clubs and all was well in 'Walterworld'!

Session Six

Walter discovers the 'Holy Grail of Delegation'

"How are things going now?" asked the Doctor.

"Pretty good... for my own work at least..." replied Walter finishing in an unfinished kind of manner.

"But?" asked the Doctor.

"Well, my manager's away for a month and I've been asked to cover," said Walter reluctantly.

"And?" the Doctor prompted.

"The bit I'm finding hard is delegating," confessed Walter. "I'm struggling to figure out who to give what. Everyone is so busy... so I've been taking on most of it myself. I'm back to long hours again... Just when I thought everything was working okay."

"And how is your communication going?" asked the Doctor relating back to the previous session.

"Not bad," admitted Walter. "I've purposely been using the whiteboard approach but it seems I have twice as much on it as everyone else! It's a bit embarrassing so I don't really put everything of mine on the list."

"So you know what your team is doing but they don't know everything you have on?" the Doctor summarised.

"I don't want to burden them," cried Walter. "And, if I'm honest, I don't want them to know I'm not coping very well with delegation!"

"So what stops you delegating well?" asked the Doctor.

"Firstly, everyone is busy," said Walter. "So I'd be adding to their work."

"Okay," the Doctor nodded. "And did your manager do that with you? Add to your workload?"

"Yes, I guess so," said Walter slowly as he gazed at the floor.

"And did you cope?" asked the Doctor?

"Eventually… with your help!"

"And could you now help others to cope?" asked the Doctor, somewhere between coaching and coaxing.

"By sharing ideas that we have explored here… yes I could," owned Walter.

"Okay, here's the deal," said the Doctor, leaning forward in a conspiratorial manner. "Most people have reasons for not delegating although when it comes down to it, *they're really excuses!*"

"What if they don't have anyone to delegate to?" challenged Walter. "Or sometimes I think it's quicker to do it myself!"

"If someone really doesn't have anyone that they manage, then delegation might be a moot point... lovely word 'moot'!" said the Doctor with an air of distraction. "If they don't have anyone to delegate a particular task to because no-one knows how to do the task... then there needs to be some training and coaching put in place within the team. This is the same with the 'quicker to do it myself' defence... If it really *is* a one-off task then that may be true... but how often is it genuinely one-off? In the long run, it will actually be quicker to train someone to delegate to."

"I know... I guess I use that excuse when I'm being reactive," admitted Walter.

"Okay, so that's a nice difference between reactive and responsive," said the Doctor. "Responsive entails building a list of others you can brief and delegate to. If something suddenly arrives on your desk... you then know who to give it to."

"Fair enough," Walter conceded.

"For your interest, here's a summary list of reasons people sometimes give for not delegating:

Excuse	Solution
It's quicker to do it myself.	If it is genuinely a one off task then fair enough... otherwise it will be quicker to train and delegate.
They won't do it properly. It's too risky. It might go wrong. I'd get blamed. I lose control over the finished result.	Train them properly! Manage the risk by controlling how much authority you give them.
They might do it better than me!	Congratulate yourself on how well you trained them... and now learn from them!
I don't want to burden them. They are already busy.	If necessary, let them put something else to one side whilst they do this task.
What if they say no? I don't want to create upset.	Be fair in how much you delegate. Get clear about whether (a) you **need** them to do it (which conveys a sense of urgency to which is not really an option) or (b) you **would like** them to do it (which suggests a 'development opportunity' where they have more choice in the matter).
I enjoy doing it and don't want to let it go.	Don't just delegate things that are not enjoyable! Find something else for yourself that you enjoy doing!
It doesn't really occur to me to delegate.	Take a longer term view and put a plan together. Build this into the other person's objectives and schedule into your own diary to make sure it happens.

"If necessary, you might need to sell the idea of delegation to yourself!" continued the Doctor. "What do you imagine are some of the benefits of delegation... to you and to them?"

"Well," said Walter thoughtfully. "The benefits to them? I guess it gives them something different to do... Helps them learn a new task and perhaps a new skill... Gives them an insight into my role and prepares them for next steps. And to me? It could free me up to do other stuff!"

"Indeed, agreed the Doctor. "It also gives you time to think strategically or to take on some of *your* manager's tasks... that way you are learning the next level up and preparing yourself for progression!"

"I suppose," agreed Walter.

"Having said all of the above," noted the Doctor. "There are some things as a manager that you *shouldn't* delegate, for example, management level duties like appraisals and personnel policies. In addition, things that require your authority and of course 'people management', you know... like encouragement, motivation, guidance and direction!"

"Yes, that's true," agreed Walter. "And helpful too."

"Good," said the Doctor. Then he began to tap on the desk as if creating an impromptu drumroll. "Now let's get to the *Holy Grail of Delegation!*"

"Ooooh!" cooed Walter, joining in on the act.

"Now I presume that you know what tasks you'd like to delegate?" the Doctor asked.

"Yes, I think so," said Walter. "There *are* a set of things that don't have to be done by me… I just couldn't figure out who to give them to… or how! But now that I think about it, I *do* know who… *and* I can spread the tasks out fairly around the team."

"So let's start with the two key considerations," began the Doctor. "Number one: 'the organisational impact of the task' and number two: 'the experience of the person for this task'."

"What do you mean by 'organisational impact'?" asked Walter.

"Okay, think of a task," began the Doctor. "Now… how far does the implementation and result of that task spread across, up and down the organisation? What is the ripple effect? Alternatively, ask yourself: 'What would happen if this task didn't get done, didn't meet the deadline or didn't get done properly?' What effect would that have within and outside the organisation?"

"You're talking about the 'What would hit the fan?' question again!" said Walter.

"Ah yes… I'd forgotten about that!" laughed the Doctor. "The greater the ripple effect and/or cost resulting from a set-back, the higher potential risk it is to the business and hence a higher organisational impact."

"Right..." said Walter, processing the Doctor's response. "And then figuring out the experience of the person should be easy enough."

"Yes," agreed the Doctor. "And remember, this means their experience *for this specific task*... not just generally. Otherwise we may fall into the trap of thinking: 'Oh they are good at this kind of thing'... which could lead to us 'dumping' the task on them."

"Sounds nasty!" said Walter.

"Have you ever been given a task to do but then not really understood what you are meant to be doing with it?" the Doctor asked.

"Oh yes!" Walter confirmed. "Quite a lot!"

"And how did *that* feel?" asked the Doctor.

"Um... annoying... a bit embarrassing..." considered Walter. "I gave myself a bit of a hard time, thinking that I should know how to do it. I think it knocked my confidence a bit. I ended up putting it in my in-tray and kind of 'forgetting' about it!"

"So!" exclaimed the Doctor. "Dumping a task on someone, i.e. giving them a task they are not fully trained to do, can lead to a loss of confidence and a case of procrastination!"

"Oh yes... dear old procrastination!"

"In addition, you will want to *know* that they have experience and can do the task well," continued the Doctor. "Just because they tell you they can, it doesn't mean they'll do it how you need it doing. The question is: 'What do you know about their *track record* with this task?'"

"So what do you do if someone *says* they can do it but you haven't seen them or their results?" asked Walter. "Then you don't *really* know... you are taking their word for it."

"You might want to talk it through," the Doctor responded. "Be straight with them. They may well have experience but they may not know how *you* need it done. And you also need to *know that they know* so ask them to give you an idea as to how they would do it."

"Okay. And what if they don't actually have the experience?"

"Ah, yes, we'll come back to that," said the Doctor. "But for now you have the idea of the *impact of a task* and the *experience of the person for the task*. This will tell you how much *authority* you can give them to do that task."

"What do you mean by 'authority'?" asked Walter.

"Ooh, good question!" said the Doctor excitedly. "Perhaps the easiest answer is *'decision power'*. What do they have the freedom to do and to change... how far can they go? This, in essence, is the core of empowerment... *freedom within boundaries*. You set the boundaries depending on the level of authority you are giving them. In practical terms, the amount of authority you give will tell you:

a. How much communication do you need with them about this task?
b. How much flexibility/freedom do they have to adapt the way it is done?
c. What do you want them to do if problems arise?

It could be argued that these three areas determine the main risks of delegation."

"What do you mean?" asked Walter.

"Okay," the Doctor responded. "So the main risks of delegation are things like: communication breaking down, people going off and doing things their own way which means they come back with something other than what you wanted. Alternatively, a problem might arise and it gets mishandled, causing further, bigger problems."

"Fair enough," said Walter, "But I'm getting a bit overwhelmed with terms and ideas here... how do you link all of this up?"

"Okay," said the Doctor, taking a breath. "The impact of the task and experience of the person will determine the level of authority. This in turn will determine communication level, flexibility and problem resolution."

"Right," said Walter, nodding. "Can you give me an example?"

"Of course!" said the Doctor. "If the task is lower impact and the person is experienced you can give them a higher level of authority. In real terms this means you should require less communication, give them more freedom and let them solve problems... whilst still keeping you informed."

"So low impact plus high experience means higher authority," Walter summarised, jotting down some notes.

"Alternatively," said the Doctor. "If the impact is higher and experience is lower, it doesn't mean you can't delegate. You *can* delegate but you will need to have:
- more planned communication... like updates,
- limited flexibility... for example: 'I need you to do it this particular way and follow the procedure' and
- limited problem resolution... you might say 'if you get any issues, please talk to me about it before moving on.'"

"Isn't delegating a 'high impact/low experience' task way too risky?" asked Walter.

"That's a decision you will need to make," conceded the Doctor. "It is still important to train the person and coach them... to help them build knowledge, skill, experience and confidence. Here's a model if it helps:"

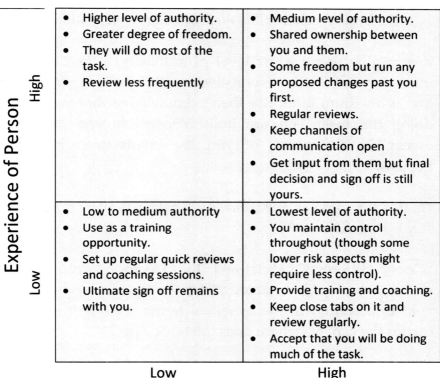

	Low	High
High	• Higher level of authority. • Greater degree of freedom. • They will do most of the task. • Review less frequently	• Medium level of authority. • Shared ownership between you and them. • Some freedom but run any proposed changes past you first. • Regular reviews. • Keep channels of communication open • Get input from them but final decision and sign off is still yours.
Low	• Low to medium authority • Use as a training opportunity. • Set up regular quick reviews and coaching sessions. • Ultimate sign off remains with you.	• Lowest level of authority. • You maintain control throughout (though some lower risk aspects might require less control). • Provide training and coaching. • Keep close tabs on it and review regularly. • Accept that you will be doing much of the task.

Experience of Person (vertical axis: Low / High)

Impact of Task (horizontal axis: Low / High)

After looking at the diagram, Walter concluded: "So you would tell them: when you will review it... how much flexibility, or not, that they have... and what to do if problems arise? I can see this could be useful in terms of managing the risk... I still keep control of *how* we work together."

"Good," said the Doctor. "Now another part of delegation is understanding '*responsibility*'. This is different to authority since responsibility means: 'who owns the task and/or who is doing it?' To make this easier:

The level of responsibility must equal the level of authority.

If you give them a low level of authority... then don't tell them they are totally responsible for it! If you are giving them low or medium authority then acknowledge that *you are both* doing the task. You are both responsible and have joint ownership since both of you are involved in making it happen."

"Is this the same as *accountability*?" asked Walter, then added: "Or is that different?"

"Oooh, different!" exclaimed the Doctor. "Accountability means 'who is able to account' for the task and 'who may be held to account'. In metaphorical terms we might say: 'who carries the can' or 'where does the buck stop'?"

"You mean 'who gets the blame if it all goes wrong'!" laughed Walter.

"It might be..." agreed the Doctor. "Though it may help to think of it in neutral terms. The balance is that the person accountable also gets the credit and acclaim for success. If you are delegating a task, you can delegate authority and responsibility but accountability stays with you."

"Oooh," wailed Walter in his best spooky voice. "Scary monsters!"

"So make sure you apply the *Holy Grail of Delegation* and manage it effectively!" smiled the Doctor.

"I guess so," agreed Walter.

"Okay," said the Doctor, keen to move the conversation on. "There will of course be other things you'll want to know when delegating. Here's an overview of some key considerations, especially for you from *The Secret Tome of Delegation!*"

"I think you are making some of this up," smiled Walter as the Doctor handed him a page from a workbook. Walter took a moment to look it over:"

Key Considerations from 'The Secret Tome of Delegation'

PREPARATION STAGE

ABOUT TASK	ABOUT 'DELEGATEE'	ABOUT DELEGATOR
❑ What? Why? How?	❑ Who?	❑ Set time aside in diary to delegate
❑ Specific, measurable brief with steps and deadlines/ milestones	❑ Availability?	
	❑ Experience?	❑ Do I need them to do it or want/like them to do it?
	❑ Authority level?	
❑ Resources needed (skills/time/equipment etc.)?	❑ Resources available (skill/time/ equipment etc.)?	❑ Contingency, e.g. if they can't/ won't do it?
❑ Impact level?	❑ Training/practise needed?	
❑ Communication level?		❑ Make sure you understand the brief. If it has been passed on to you, ask questions so you do understand.
❑ Priority level?	❑ Likely motivation & commitment?	
❑ Likelihood of changes in task or priority?	❑ What else are they working on?	
❑ Complexity? Does it need breaking down?		

BRIEFING STAGE

❑ Explain…   clear information about the task (what, when, why and how).
               what they are responsible for and give them appropriate authority.
               what has been done already. Identify who can help.
               the possibility of change.

❑ Agree…   communication level and procedure, review dates and timings.
               what to do if problems arise.
               priority level and degree of flexibility.

❑ Give them time to think/digest (if necessary)
❑ Check understanding and confidence
❑ Inform the appropriate others what you have delegated and to whom

MONITORING STAGE

❑ Keep your eyes and door open, but your hands off.
❑ Communicate and review at the level you agreed and adjust as necessary.
❑ Motivate them and encourage.
❑ Support them as necessary.
❑ Keep a written record (e.g. action points).

COMPLETION STAGE

❑ Final review – what went well and what changes would they/you recommend?
❑ Thank them.
❑ Acknowledge, celebrate and credit.

"Ah, now this is helpful…" Walter said, nodding with understanding. "There's quite a lot here but most of it seems to be general good practice."

"Indeed," said the Doctor. "And they are suggestive as opposed to absolute. It's your choice as to what you focus on here. Different situations may require different considerations. Ultimately, make sure you agree to what you have agreed to, particularly the actions, deadlines, priorities and, of course, when and how often you want to communicate."

"I just thought of something," said Walter, a question dawning on his face. "What do you do if someone doesn't want to do it and says 'no'!?"

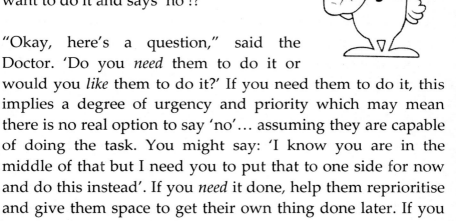

"Okay, here's a question," said the Doctor. 'Do you *need* them to do it or would you *like* them to do it?' If you need them to do it, this implies a degree of urgency and priority which may mean there is no real option to say 'no'... assuming they are capable of doing the task. You might say: 'I know you are in the middle of that but I need you to put that to one side for now and do this instead'. If you *need* it done, help them reprioritise and give them space to get their own thing done later. If you would *like* them to do it, this implies that there is more of a choice. 'Like them to' suggests it is a 'development opportunity' that they could take on or not. So think about what you are actually asking and use the appropriate language."

"What if they are still resistant?" persevered Walter.

"If you can, find out what's causing the resistance," suggested the Doctor. "Is it lack of time or overload of work? If so, can you remove or reschedule something for them? Is it lack of knowledge, skill or confidence? If so, train them and support them in their learning process. Or you might do the task yourself and delegate something else to them that you would have been doing otherwise. Is it due to the fact that they don't like doing that thing or find it boring? If so, balance this with things they *do* like. Alternatively, you might look at who else could do the task. Is there someone else who *does* enjoy doing it? If it's a dull task, make sure there's a perceived fairness by rotating the task around the team."

"Good," said Walter. Then after a moment's thought added: "Oh... and when it comes to finding out how people are getting on with a task, I have someone in my team who responds with a single word... 'Fine'. That's all they say! How on earth do you deal with that?"

"Remember that there are different personalities out there," said the Doctor. "Some people hear the word 'how' in a question and respond with a one word answer. It is as if they don't seem to do 'evaluation' questions. Instead, you might want to ask a 'process' question, for example: 'where are you up to with that task?' This way you are asking them what stage they are at in the process. This is usually easier for them to answer. If they answer 'nearly there' then try: 'okay *specifically* where are you up to?'"

"Yes... that might work," considered Walter. "They seem to like working on their own. But they really like to know the steps to getting something done. You are right... they are very process driven."

"Whilst we're talking of different personalities," said the Doctor. "I do recommend having a template or working example of what you are looking for. I mentioned this in a previous session, but it does seem to work for all the different personalities. It gives them clarity and boundaries to work within. It shows them what result you expect."

"And what about when people keep coming back to you and acting as if they don't know what to do next?" Walter moaned. "Sometimes they ask questions that I know they have answers to. They've had training and they've done the task before... it's as if they are looking for an excuse not to do it."

"Okay, so the first thing is 'what *not* to do'... or at least 'what to avoid if possible'," said the Doctor. "If someone brings you something they are working on and they have a question about it, avoid saying things like 'leave it with me' or 'just leave it on my desk and I'll look into it'. As soon as you do this you have taken the task off them and potentially disempowered them. Maybe all they want is to check something with you or get a specific answer or some advice. It can be very frustrating when a manager takes a task off you and adds it to the pile on their in-tray!"

"Yes, that's true," agreed Walter. "My old manager used to do that. I hated it."

"Okay, so if someone has a question, it could mean a number of things," the Doctor began. "Is it a while since they did the task and so they have forgotten part of it, or do they want to double check they are doing the right thing? Alternatively, they may be asking because they genuinely don't know. If it's a case of the latter, then run through it with them again. If you think they do know really, then ask some questions. Here are some classic coaching questions to help them come up with their own answers. First help them establish their current state and their desired state:

Where are you up to now?

Where are you wanting to get to? What is your outcome?

"These questions help them establish the gap between where they are and where they want to get to. It also helps you understand what their issue is and may give you an indicator as to whether they know what they are meant to be doing! Then you can get them to elicit possible solutions:

How might you get there? What could you do?

"If they answer this question and the answer seems good, they were simply making sure they had it right. By saying 'sounds fine to me', you will probably help them build confidence. If they can't answer or give you something completely outlandish, then you might need to tell them the answer or show them how to do it."

"Excellent!" said Walter. "I think that will do it… I'm ready to delegate!"

"Excellent indeed," echoed the Doctor. "Now go and *be brilliant...*"

Walter's Notes

Check my reasons if I'm not delegating... are they reasonable or simply an excuse?

Remember that not only does delegation help me... but it should also benefit them.

When delegating, consider the Holy Grail questions:

- What is the impact of the task?
- What is the experience of the person for the task?

Don't dump tasks on people. Make sure they have the training, experience and support. Also let them know why the task needs doing and why the deadline is important. Talk them through the details and be clear about the required outcome, the deadline and the priority level of the task.

Give them appropriate levels of authority (decision power) and responsibility (ownership).

Delegation Plan: Questions
- What could I delegate? Impact of task (1-5)?
- Who to? Experience of Person for this task (1-5)?
- Level of Authority (& therefore Responsibility)?
- What else do I need to consider? (See the 'Secret Tome of Delegation'!)

Sixth Slice

Who Stole My Pie

A Final Slice of Pie

Who Stole My Pie

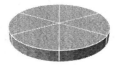

A month or so later, as Walter was purchasing his daily pie from the 'Pie-in-ere', the pie-shop-keeper gave Walter a big grin.

"For a little while now I have wanted to thank you, Walter," said the shop-keeper with a small tear in his eye.

"What on earth for?" replied Walter, a little perplexed.

The Maker of Pies explained to Walter that three months previous, the shop had almost gone out of business. But now it was flourishing.

Fame had spread way beyond Walter's company, with people telling people telling people telling people... There had even been some articles in the local papers with a visit from a couple of television crews... who then became customers too.

"And so Walter," said the maker of pies in a voice most formal and official. "In this shop, from this day forth, you shall be known as the 'Pied Piper'."

He shook Walter's hand most vigorously and grinned again. Then, he gave Walter a scroll which read:

Who Stole My Pie

To the Pied Piper.

For services rendered, you will be due one pie each day at no charge.

With our greatest thanks.

The Pie-in-Ere

Final Slice

Who Stole My Pie

Notes & Further Reading

Session 3

1. Covey, S. (2004) *The Seven Habits of Highly Effective People*, Simon & Schuster.
2. The 'next smallest step' approach was developed by John Overdurf and Julie Silverthorn in their HNLP Coaching models.
3. Bertie Wooster, of 'Jeeves and Wooster' fame, is a fictional character invented by P.G. Wodehouse.

Session 4

1. For those that are interested, the Doctor's formula for working out the Proactive/Reactive timings is based on the percentage of time spent actually doing the proactive work (100/Proactive%) converted into minutes (*60):

   *100 / Proactive% * 60*

About the Author

About Joe Cheal

Joe is a partner in the GWiz Learning Partnership. He has been involved in the field of management and organisational development since 1993. In focusing his training, coaching and consultancy experience within the business environment, he has worked with a broad range of organisational cultures, helping thousands of people revolutionise the way they work with others.

He holds an MSc in Organisational Development and Neuro Linguistic Technologies (his MSc dissertation was an exploration into 'social paradox'), a degree in Philosophy and Psychology and diplomas in Coaching and Psychotherapy.

Joe is an NLP Master Trainer who enjoys learning new things... by exploring diverse fields of science, philosophy and psychology and then integrating these 'learnings'. He is the author of *Solving Impossible Problems*, the co-author of *The Model Presenter* and is the creator and editor of the ANLP Journal: *Acuity*.

He is a regular speaker at conferences and groups. He can be contacted at: joe@gwiztraining.com.

The GWiz Learning Partnership

The GWiz Learning Partnership is a consultancy that specialises in inspiring the natural potential of organisations, leadership, management and individuals through OD, L&D and Executive Coaching.

We work with clients from a broad range of sectors and aim to work in partnership with our clients, enhancing the profile of leadership, learning and development in our client's organisation.

Since 1993 we have experience of working with thousands of people from many organisations including:

Aeroflex, Amnesty International, ARA (Aircraft Research Association), Astra Zeneca & AstraTech, Autoglass, Avondale, Balfour Beatty, Bedford Borough Council, Central Bedfordshire, Beds Health, Beds Magistrates Courts Committee, Belron, Bio-Products Laboratories (BPL), Birdlife and Plantlife, British Gas, BT, Calderdale Council, Cambridge City Council, Cambridge University Press, Camelot, Cellnet, Central Bedfordshire, Church Conservation Trust, Cranfield University, Dixons Stores Group International, Emmaus Village Carlton, GSK, Herts Magistrates Courts Committee, Hertsmere Borough Council, Inland Revenue, J. Murphy & Sons, Langley Search & Selection, Lockheed Martin, London Borough of Camden, Luton Borough Council, Mylan, Newham Council, North Herts District Council, OAG, Olympic Blinds, RSPB, Sainsbury's, Santander, Serco, Shepherd Stubbs Recruitment, Staverton Park Conference Centre, The Assessment Network, Tesco, University of Hertfordshire, Welwyn Hatfield Borough Council, Welwyn Hatfield Community Housing Trust, Willmott Dixon, The Wine Society.

The GWiz Learning Partnership offers a range of consultancy services including:
- Change management, OD and L&D consultancy
- Courses
- Executive coaching and skills coaching
- Facilitation and team development
- Myers Briggs profiling and Emotional Intelligence testing
- ILM accredited qualifications
- Qualifications in NLP
- GWizzlers ('bite-size' sessions)

Our courses and topics include:

LEADERSHIP DEVELOPMENT
Change Management
Coaching Performance
Coaching Skills for Managers
The Complete Leader: Inspirational & Practical
Delegate!
Feedback for Effectiveness
Leadership in Action
Making Meetings Work
Management Development Programme
Managing Home-Workers
Managing People Successfully
Mentoring 1: Becoming a Mentor
Mentoring 2: Developing Further Mentor Skills
Motivate!
Project Leadership
The Supportive Manager
Team Building and Development

RESULTS AND RELATIONSHIPS
Advanced Customer Care
Assertiveness: Clarity and Focus
Building Partnerships
Communication
Conflict Resolution
Customer Care
Dealing with Aggression
Dealing with Difficult People
Handling Conflict in Meetings
Influence and Persuasion
Listening Completely
Magic of Mediation
Negotiation Skills
Rapport
Understanding Personalities

IN FRONT OF THE AUDIENCE
Advanced Presentation Skills
The Essential Presenter
Persuasive Presentations
Train the Trainer

PERSONAL IMPACT
Career & Profile Development
Coping with Change
Dealing With Pressure
Innovation: Getting Creative
Lift Off: Personal Development
Making Your Life Work 4U: Confidence
Managing Your Performance
Networking Skills
Personal Power
Self Awareness & Personal Development
Staying Positively Happy
Stress Management
Time Management

EXECUTIVE DEVELOPMENT
Advanced Negotiation Skills
Becoming a Mentor
Beyond Selling
Business Hypnotix
Executive Leadership in Action
Making NLP Work
Managing Tensions
Organisational Development
Organisational Politics
Storytelling in Business
Strategic Change Management
Troubleshooting: Problem Resolution
Working with Transactional Analysis

HR SKILLS FOR MANAGERS
Appraisal
Capability & Disciplinary
Controlling Absence
Dealing with Poor Performance
Introduction to Counselling
Managing Difficult People
Recruitment Selection & Interviewing
Tackling Bullying & Harassment

CPD FOR HR PROFESSIONALS
Building Working Partnerships
Influencing the Organisation
Raising the Profile of HR

Have a look at our website: www.gwiztraining.com or contact us at info@gwiztraining.com.

135

Training in Neuro-linguistic Programming (NLP)

NLP (Neuro-linguistic Programming) could be described as the psychology of excellence and the science of change. Through understanding more about how the mind/brain works (neuro) and how language affects us (linguistic), a practitioner is able to initiate and sustain change (programming) on a personal, interpersonal and organisational level.

NLP was designed originally to model excellence. By establishing exactly how someone achieves something, excellence can be modelled, taught to someone else and repeated again and again. From this starting point, over the last thirty years, an array of processes, concepts and techniques have been developed to enable you to:

- become more resourceful in managing attitudes, thoughts, emotions, behaviours and beliefs
- relate to others easily and effortlessly,
- understand how language and its use has a direct impact on your state, your brain and your success in communicating with others.

In addition to all this, as a GWiz NLP practitioner, you will learn techniques designed to help you develop your own skills and help others develop theirs. The principles will be introduced conversationally and with activities throughout the course allowing you to learn on many levels consciously and unconsciously.

As NLP Master Trainers we offer the complete three levels of certified NLP courses throughout the year:

- NLP 101
- NLP Diploma
- NLP Practitioner
- NLP Master Practitioner
- NLP Trainer's Training

If you are interested in personal and professional development and would like to more about NLP, have a look at our website: www.gwiznlp.com or contact us: info@gwiznlp.com.

Lightning Source UK Ltd.
Milton Keynes UK
UKOW04f1445250914

239185UK00001B/28/P